The
MUPPET
SHOW
BOOK

Introduction

Hi-ho, Kermit the Frog here welcoming you to the Muppet Show Book. What you are about to be amused and amazed by are some of the classic pieces from our first two seasons on TV. Now, you're probably asking why these pieces were chosen, and others were not. Well, we carefully assembled all the scripts, then we turned out the lights and threw them up in . . . *(enter Piggy)*

Kermit the Frog

MP: Oh, Kerm-ie . . . before we go any further, I think everyone would like to know why the STAR of this book, *moi,* does not appear until page 40? Don't you think we should remedy that? Or, DO YOU WANT TO GET FLATTENED BETWEEN THE PAGES?

K: Er . . . You can't 'cause this book is so fascinating no one can possibly close it and . . .

F: Hey man what are we doing in a *book?* The only notes a book has is footnotes* and you can't hear them.

J: Oh, wow! Is that why frogs don't have ears?

Z: Decidedly un-harmonic, man.

Miss Piggy

UNHARMONIC!
UNHARMONIC!

SGT. FLOYD PEPPER   DR. TEETH   ZOOT   *Janice*   Animal

*Footnotes:

It's time to play the mu-sic,   It's time to light the light,   It's time to raise the cur-tain on The Mup-pet Show to-night.

WALDORF   **STATLER**

S: Do you think they'll be funnier in print than they were on TV?

W: I wouldn't make book on it!

F: Say! Speaking of books, I've got a story you'll get a bang out of. It seems . . .

FOZZIE BEAR

CH: Did somebody say "Bang"?

HA HA HA HA HA HA

CRAZY HARRY

B A N G

K: Well, that about does it for the introduction. I hope things go better with the book.

Good grief.

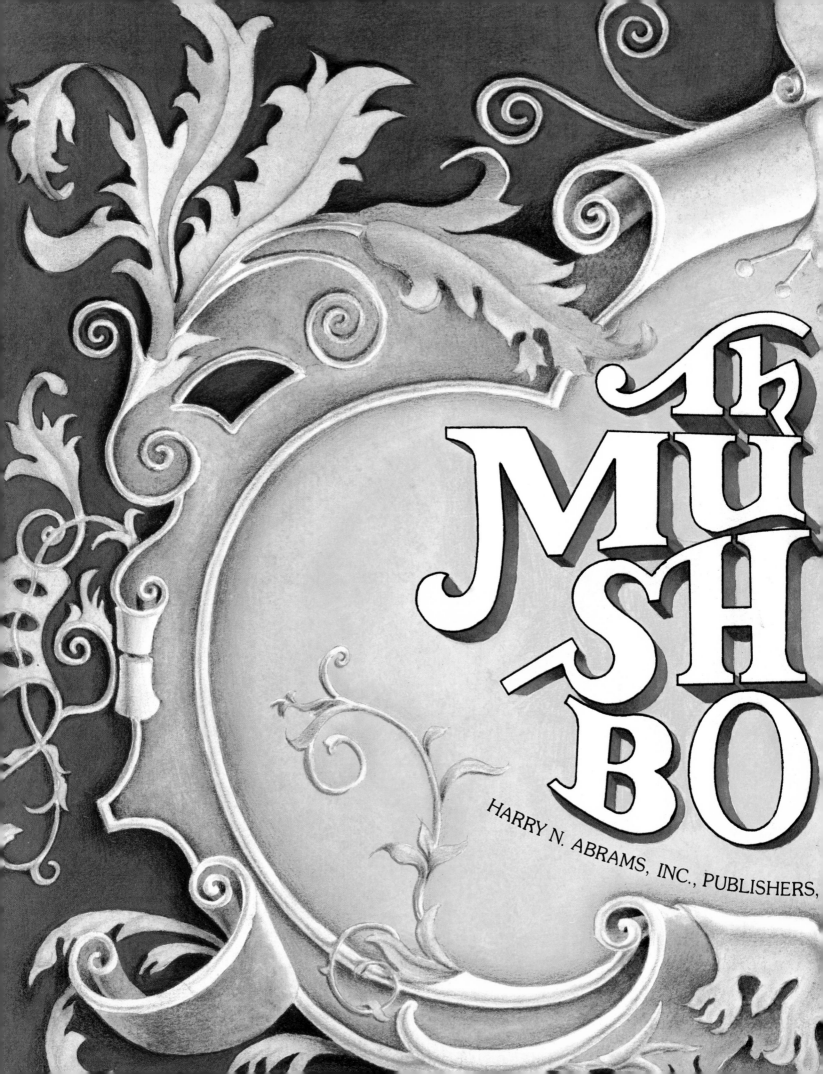

Th
MU
SH
BO

HARRY N. ABRAMS, INC., PUBLISHERS,

e PPET OW OK

NEW YORK

The material in this book is based on material which appeared
during the first two seasons of The Muppet Show

PRODUCERS

Jack Burns   Jim Henson

DIRECTORS

Peter Harris   Philip Casson

WRITERS

Jack Burns   Jerry Juhl

Marc London, Joseph A. Bailey

Jim Henson

and

Don Hinkley

CREATIVE CONSULTANT

Frank Oz

SCENIC DESIGNERS

David Chandler, Brian Holgate, Malcolm Stone

EXECUTIVE PRODUCER FOR HENSON ASSOCIATES

David Lazer

Layout and illustrations by TUDOR BANUS
Assisted by Ariel Moscovici and Melissa Zorn
Project coordinator: Nai Y. Chang
Editorial consultant: Betty Ballantine
Library of Congress Catalogue Card Number: 78-60710
Standard Book Number: 0-8109-1328-3
© Henson Associates, Inc., 1978

It's The Muppet Show Book...

starring Jim Henson's Muppets!

It's time to play the mu-sic, it's time to light the light,

It's time to raise the cur-tain on The Mup-pet Show to-night.

It's time to put on make-up, it's time to dress up right,

You'll see the strangest crea-tures on The Mup-pet Show to-night.

THE NEW GO-FER

Scooter: *(entering):*
Hi! Are you Kermit the Frog?

Kermit: Er. Yer. Yeah.

S: I'm Scooter.

K: Cute . . . Cute name.

S: I'm your new go-fer.

K: Gopher? . . . er, no, we have frogs and pigs and chickens around here . . . but we've never had a gopher . Matter of fact, you don't even *look* like a gopher.

S: Yeah, well, you don't understand. You *see* I'm your new *go-fer.* I'll go fer coffee, I'll go fer sandwiches, I'll go fer anything you need.

K: Oh . . . I see . . .

S: And I work real cheap and I've got plenty of ideas for your theater and I'll start tonight, OK?

K: Er, l-listen kid . . . I'm sorry but you're too young, you don't have any experience and I don't have any money for it in the budget.

S: Yeah, and my uncle owns this theater.

K: You start today, get me a cup of coffee . . . your salary is twenty a week. OK, everybody, *(Into intercom)* stand by for the next number . . .

S: Could you make it twenty-five?

K: ARE YOU KIDDING?? I CAN'T AFFORD IT!!

S: Gee, my uncle will be really disappointed.

K: How about thirty?

S: Hey Kermit, here's your coffee . . . OH!

EEEYOW!

S: Oh, hot, eh? Is that the way you like it?

Um, too much sugar

S: Well, anyway, I just found this fantastic new act.

K: Er, Scooter, I don't have time right now on the show for a new act.

S: Uh, that's too bad. I found it in my uncle's office. It's his favorite act.

K: Er, what's the name of the new act?

S: Oh, they're called "Mahna Mahna and the Two Snowths." They're fantastic! FANTASTIC! They're out of sight.

K: And they're your uncle's favorite act? Hey! Mahna Mahna, Snowths, you're on.

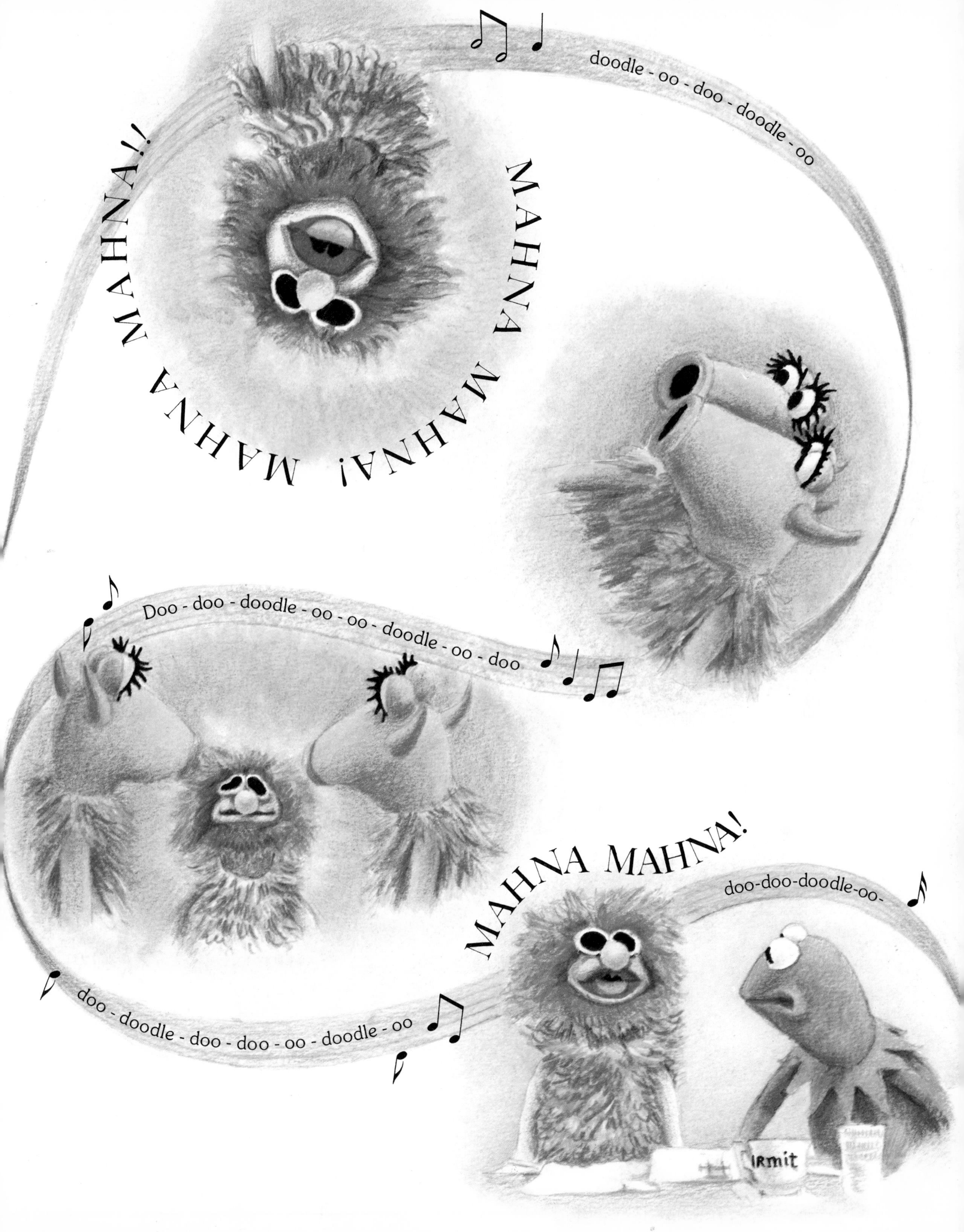
MAHNA MAHNA! MAHNA MAHNA!!
doodle - oo - doo - doodle - oo
Doo - doo - doodle - oo - oo - doodle - oo - doo
MAHNA MAHNA!
doo-doo-doodle-oo-
doo - doodle - doo - doo - oo - doodle - oo

Kermit: Er, George, George, come here.

George (The Janitor)
I'm busy.

K: Come here. Have you met Scooter? This is Scooter . . . he's our new go-fer . . . so if you need anything around here, you know . . . *(exits)*

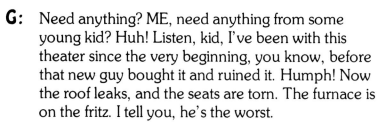

G: Need anything? ME, need anything from some young kid? Huh! Listen, kid, I've been with this theater since the very beginning, you know, before that new guy bought it and ruined it. Humph! Now the roof leaks, and the seats are torn. The furnace is on the fritz. I tell you, he's the worst.

S: He's my uncle.

G: He's the BEST. What's a theater without problems? Right? Your uncle's got a good head on his shoulders . . .

unlike some people around here.

30¢ REWARD
KID FOZ

¢ ¢ ¢

Sheriff Fast-Draw, Bullet County, New York

Rowlf

I've been playing the saloon piano in Snake City fer three years. It was the roughest town in the West. I mean, we had some mean customers! After three years I thought I'd seen it all. I'd seen the Clanton Brothers, the Younger Brothers, the James Brothers . . . not to mention the Osmond Brothers. But when Kid Fozzie hit town, I knew I hadn't seen nothing.

ALL RIGHT EVERYBODY REACH FOR THE FLOOR!

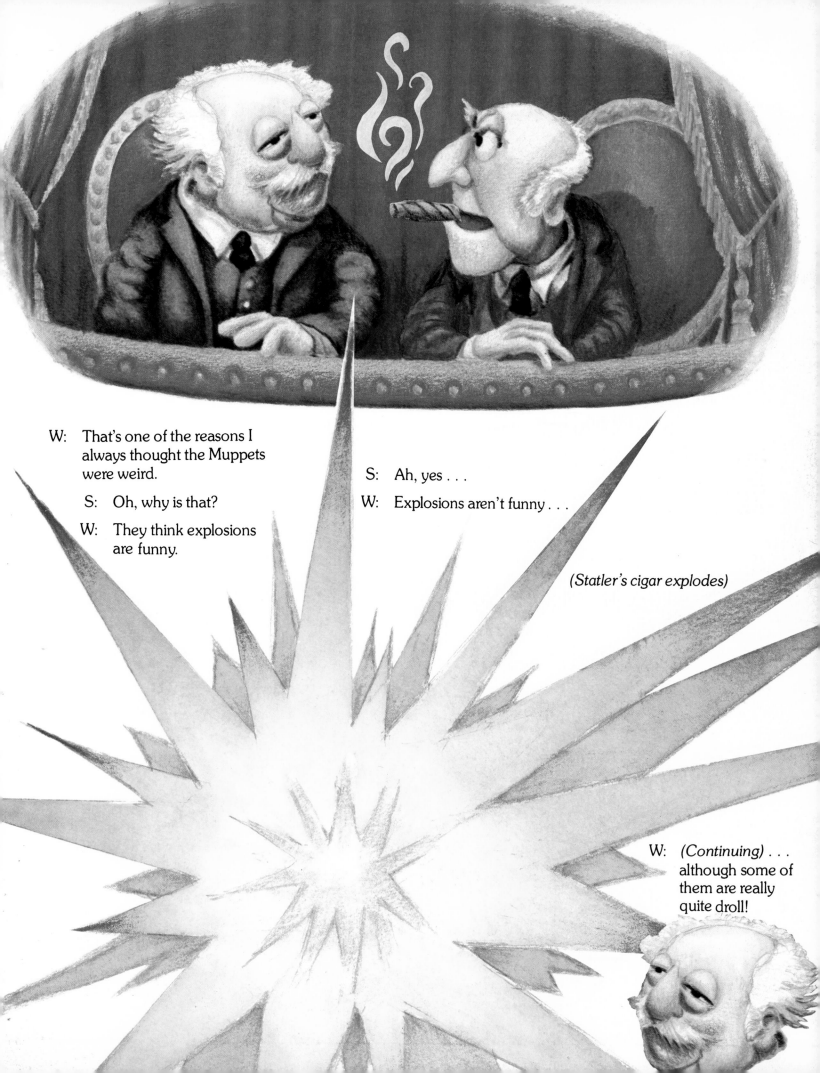

W: That's one of the reasons I always thought the Muppets were weird.

S: Oh, why is that?

W: They think explosions are funny.

S: Ah, yes . . .

W: Explosions aren't funny . . .

(Statler's cigar explodes)

W: *(Continuing)* . . . although some of them are really quite droll!

ROBOT FROG

Kermit: Scooter? Scooter, what is this?

Scooter: It's a crate.

K: I can see it's a crate, but who's responsible for it?

S: Oh, I am.

K: Scooter! What makes you think you can bring a crate into the backstage?

S: My uncle who owns the theater . . .

K: And a very nice crate it is, too. Ah, may I ask you what's in it?

S: Sure . . . go ahead.

K: WHAT'S IN IT?

S: Well, it's a mechanical, wind-up TV show host.

K: A mechanical, wind-up TV show host?

S: Right!

K: That is the *dumbest,* the *craziest,* most *ridiculous* idea you have ever had!

(Crate opens and inside is a duplicate of Kermit)

K: Aaah! Scooter, you're out of your mind!

ROBOT :   Be careful, frog. His uncle owns the theater.

(Robot pushes Kermit into crate and slams the cover shut)

AH HAH! *click* HAW! *clack* HAH!

GONZO THE GREAT

Kermit: Let me take this opportunity to present you with our resident artist . . .

THE GREAT GONZO

Oh, thank you, thank you very much, thank you. Tonight, ladies and gentlemen, I will eat this rubber tire to the music of "The Flight of the Bumblebee." Music, maestro.

WALDORF:

He is doing it.

STATLER:

He is eating a tire!

Amazing!   Astounding!   Boring!

K: Looks like it's another wipe out for Gonzo.

Ahh, yokels.

What do they know about ART!

Kermit: Well, time soon for the handsome frog here to make one of his introductions. I will check myself and see how I look in the mirror.

K: Scooter, where did you get this ridiculous wind-up show host?

A: It was a gift from his uncle.

K: Welcome to our show . . .

AH-HAH click HAH clack HAH!

NUDITY: AN OPINION BY SAM THE EAGLE

I would just like to say a few words about nudity in the world today.
And I, for one, am just appalled by it!

Why, did you know that underneath their clothing, the entire population of the world is walking around completely naked? Is that disgusting?

And, it's not just people, although goodness knows that's bad enough. But animals too! Even cute little doggies and pussycats can't be trusted. Underneath their fur . . . absolutely naked. And, it's not just the quadrupeds either. Birds, too! Yes, beneath those fine feathers, birds wear nothing.

Nothing at all, absolu . . .
I'm a bird!!!

ROBOT in LOVE...

Miss Piggy:
Oh, light of my life, frog of my arms, at last we are alone!

Kermit:
At last *you* are alone, Piggy. I'm about to go on stage in front of a thousand people.

Oh, Oh wretched day.
For a pig in her prime to be thus scorned!
Oh, how I long to hear my love whisper sweet passion.

ROBOT FROG:

> Hiya, good lookin'. Where ya been all my life?

MP: *(Stunned)* Who me? . . . I . . . you . . . but . . .

R: Hey, listen you, how about you and me getting together and makin' some ste-e-e-am heat. Huh, snuggle bunny?

MP: Snuggle bunny? Why, ah . . .

R: Yeah. Look, let me take you away from all this. Ahh, a marriage made in heaven! A frog and a pig. We can have bouncing baby figs!

MP: *(In a daze)* Baby figs . . .

R: Sure. Let me whisper sweet nothings in your ear . . .

MP: Sweet nothings?

R: Whisper, whisper, whisper.

> *(Piggy becomes horrified)*

MP: Yuck!

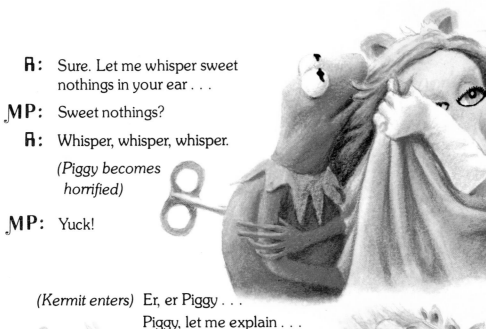

(Kermit enters) Er, er Piggy . . .
Piggy, let me explain . . .

Oh yeah?
Explain this!

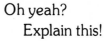 W H U M P H !

K: Hey, listen. I think you may have dented him.

MP: I don't care . . . *(does double take and faints)*

Oh well. The frog broke her fall.

T H U M P !

FURNITURE MONSTERS

Here's a Muppet Newsflash! Our newsroom has been flooded with calls today reporting that furniture all over town has been turning into monsters. Seven people have allegedly been attacked by a wandering pack of sofas at the east edge of town.

(A man sits on a hassock watching TV. The Muppet reporter is on the screen. The man looks nervously around the room.)

A dining room table set for eight reportedly ate the eight it was set for. When contacted for comment, Sheriff David Goelz assured Muppet News Central that the rumor was false. According to Goelz, there is no way for a piece of furniture to turn into a monster.

(The hassock on which the man was sitting rises up revealing angry eyes and a grinning toothy mouth.)

(Man beats hassock with rolled newspaper. Man rushes out the door with hassock and cabinet in pursuit.)

Common sense tells one that inanimate objects cannot turn into monsters. Psychologists attribute this mass hysteria to a phenomenon called "furniphobia."

(Man rushes back into room and slams door on growling and snarling furniture. He leans against door, breathing heavily.)

And that's all tonight from Muppet News! Good night!

(Man reels over to TV set. TV set grows eyes, rises up; the screen becomes a monster's mouth and eats man.)

Boy, that last item about furniture is ridiculous . . . Hey, what's happening . . . Help!

HELP! A A I E E

PIGS IN SPACE

When last we left the spaceship Swinetrek,
it was drifting aimlessly in space due to
loss of power in the steering mechanism.

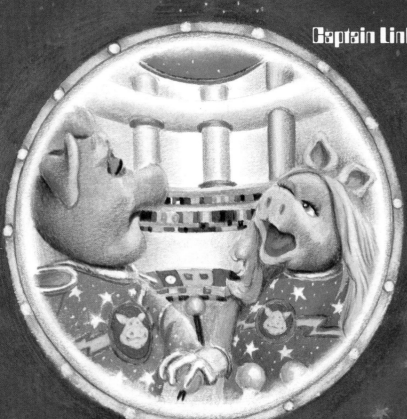

DR. JULIUS STRANGEPORK: Mm. Are you sure we've lost power in our steering mechanism, Link?

Captain Link Hogthrob: I'm afraid so, Doctor.

MP: Try that one.

L: I already did.

MP: I didn't see you.

L: You don't have to see me. I am the Captain.

S: If Link said he tried that one, I for one believe him.

MP: Men! You all stick together. I'm going to try that control.

L: Now you stay on your own side. These are the Captain's controls.

MP: But my controls are just for the hot plate, the air-conditioning, and the stereo; they have nothing to do with steering. I'm going to try this one.

L: STOP HER!   MP: *This* works the steering . . .

. . . Or the door.

Tune in next week
and don't miss
the continuation
of "Pigs In Space"!

...and now "Veterinarian's Hospital" the continuing story of a former orthopedic surgeon gone to the dogs...

Janice:

I'm sorry I'm late, Dr. Bob, I was operating in the other booth.

Rowlf:

I know, it's the talk of the hospital. Now cut that out. Let me have the ear thing.

Miss Piggy:

Ear thing, Dr. Bob.

R: Aw, feels good . . . Stick.

G: Stick, Dr. Bob.

R: Fetch!

I: What's that all about?

R: That's my labratory retriever.

HEE HEE HEE!　　HAW HAW!　hee hee!

MP: Well, what do you think?

R: I think this man is sick. He ought to see a doctor.

MP: But, Dr. Bob, you *are* a doctor.

F: That's your opinion. I'm getting out of here.

G: You can't leave, Fozzie. Dr. Bob is the only one who can save you now.

R: She's right. I saved over five hundred last year.

F: What? Patients?

R: No . . . dollars. Of course, I also lost over a hundred pounds.

F: What, in weight?

R: No, in England.

MP: Dr. Bob, you should be ashamed of yourself. You call yourself a doctor, Dr. Bob?

R: I never call myself a doctor . . . they don't come when you call them anyway.

(Tune in next week when we'll hear Nurse Piggy say:)

MP: Dr. Bob, you've lost your patients.

R: I can't help it. I've got a short temper.

F: Can I go now?

THE BAND REVOLTS

FLOYD

Hey, Kermit! So long, man.

Kermit

But, but, Floyd . . . the show is on . . . you should be in the orchestra pit.

F: Sorry man, I'm anklin'.

K: Ankling?

F: Yeah, anklin'. You know . . . leavin'. I've come to the coda, I'm using the door marked EXIT. Like the banana in the presence of the ice cream . . . I intend to split.

K: But, but but Floyd . . . you can't just leave us.

F: Uh, listen Kermit, you're a nice little dude in your own amphibian way, but I just can't take it anymore.

K: But what's the matter?

F: It's the theme song. Kermit, you are talking to Floyd Pepper, the hippest of the hip. I mean, I have a room for life at the Home for the Chronically Groovy. And every week I have to come in here and play *(hums theme)*—DUM—Dum—Dum—dum-da—dumdum . . .

K: Nice.

F: It is embarrassingly square . . . And I don't play square.

K: Yeah. But Floyd . . . none of the other musicians have complained.

K: Hey, Animal . . . you like the theme, don't you?

K: Hey, but wait a minute, Floyd, what about the big "I Feel Pretty" number?

S: Hey, hey, wait a minute, wait a minute, the dude is right. We can't walk out on the big number.

K: Good.

S: We'll walk out *after* the big number. (Musicians all exit)

K: Whew . . . a stay of execution. I must remember to thank the warden.

i feel Pretty

feel pretty, oh, so pretty,

I feel pretty and witty and bright,

And I pity any girl who isn't me tonight.

I feel charming, oh, so charming,

It's alarming how charming I feel,

And so pretty

That I hardly can believe I'm real.

See the pretty girl in that mirror there.

Who can that attractive girl be?

Such a pretty face, such a pretty dress,

Such a pretty smile, such a pretty me!

I feel stunning and entrancing,

Feel like running and dancing for joy,

For I'm loved by a pretty wonderful boy!

FLOYD

OK, Kermit, we're anklin'.

K: Hey, but, but, wait a minute, wait a minute. Listen, if you stay, next week we'll have . . . *a new theme!*

F: Oh yeah? Well, maybe we'll stay then.

(Kermit brings Nigel in)

K: Good because your noble conductor Nigel here has offered to write a new theme.

F: We're leaving. *(They all exit)*

K: Yeah, but, but *why?*

F: *(Exiting)* He wrote the first one, man.

K: But, er, but yeah, but guys come back please!

(He rushes after them)

NIGEL: I always thought it was kind of a hip tune.

Ƨ: Hey, my friendly froggy little flipper fin.

K: Yeah.

Ƨ: Me and the gang have decided not to end our gig here.

K: Oh, good!

Ƨ: *If . . .*

K: Oh, oh . . . if *what?*

Ƨ: If *I* can write the new theme song.

K: Oh, oh well, that'll be fine with me.

Ƨ: No it won't, man.

K: Er, why not?

Ƨ: You'll hate my music. You won't understand it.

K: Now, now listen here . . . I am pretty hip too, you know!

Ƨ: Not hip enough. *Nobody* understands my music. I mean . . . *I* don't even understand it.

K: You don't?

Ƨ: If I didn't know I was a genius, I wouldn't listen to the trash I write.

K: Gee . . . I can hardly wait to hear it.

(Kermit is madly painting, trying to finish this book)

Kermit

At this rate, I'll never get done.

Scooter

What's all this green paint for, boss?

K: Er-er-er green is your uncle's favorite color, isn't it?

S: I've never heard him say that.

WINDMILLS OF YOUR MIND

I am very relaxed. I
am terribly calm
and tranquil.
I am very, very relaxed indeed—on the outside . . . but on the INSIDE!!! . . . On the inside I am spinning . . .

Like a clock whose hands are sweeping
Past the minutes of its face
Like a carousel that's turning
Running rings around the moon.
Or a carnival balloon.
Like a snowball down a mountain
On an ever spinning reel.
Never ending or beginning
Like a wheel within a wheel
...round, like a circle in a spiral

And the world is like an apple
Whirling silently in space.
Like the circles that you find
In the windmills of your mind.

Like a tunnel that you follow
To a tunnel of its own.
Down a hollow to a cavern
Where the sun has never shown.
Like a door that keeps revolving
In a half forgotten dream
Or the ripples from a pebble
Someone tosses in a stream.

Like a clock whose hands are sweeping
Past the minutes of its face
And the world is like an apple
Whirling silently in space
Like the circles that you find
In the windmills of your mind.

Keys that jingle in your pocket.
Words that jangle in your head.
Why did summer go so quickly
Was it something that you said?
Lovers walk along a shore
And leave their footprints in the sand.
Is the sound of distant drumming
Just the fingers of your hand?
Pictures hanging in a hallway
And the fragment of a song
Half remembered names and faces
But to whom do they belong?
When you knew that it was over
You were suddenly aware
That the autumn leaves were turning
To the colour of her hair.

Like a circle in a spiral,
Like a wheel within a wheel.
Never ending or beginning
On an ever spinning reel.
As the images unwind
Like the circles that you find
In the windmills of your mind.

Round, like a circle in a spiral
Like a wheel within a wheel
Never ending or beginning
On an ever spinning reel.
Like a snowball down a mountain
Or a carnival balloon.
Like a carousel that's turning
Running rings around the moon.
Like a clock whose hands are sweeping
Past the minutes of its face
And the world is like an apple
Whirling silently in space.
Like the circles that you find
In the windmills of your mind.

Like a tunnel that you follow
To a tunnel of its own
Down a hollow to a cavern
Where the sun has never shown.
Like a door that keeps revolving
In a half forgotten dream
Or the ripples from a pebble
Someone tosses in a stream.

Like a clock whose hands are sweeping
Past the minutes of its face
And the world is like an apple
Whirling silently in space
Like the circles that you find
In the windmills of your mind

In the windmills of your mind
Like the circles that you find

Keys that jingle in your pocket
Words that jangle in your head.
Why did summer go so quickly
Was it something that you said?
Lovers walk along a shore
And leave their footprints in the sand.
Is the sound of distant drumming
Just the fingers of your hand?
Pictures hanging in a hallway
And the fragment of a song.
Half remembered names and faces
But to whom do they belong?
When you knew that it was over
You were suddenly aware
That the autumn leaves were turning
To the colour of her hair.

Like a circle in a spiral
Like a wheel within a wheel
Never ending or beginning
On an ever spinning reel
As the images unwind
Like the circles that you find
In the windmills of your mind.

But on the outside I'm very calm.

AAEEAAA

STATLER: Well . . . how did you like that number?

WALDORF: Hmmm? Oh . . . I didn't notice it.

S: Didn't notice it? How is that possible? It was loud and raucous with a screaming thing running amok? Oh, how could you not notice it?

W: Well, in the future I'll try to be more observant.

S: Would you do that please.

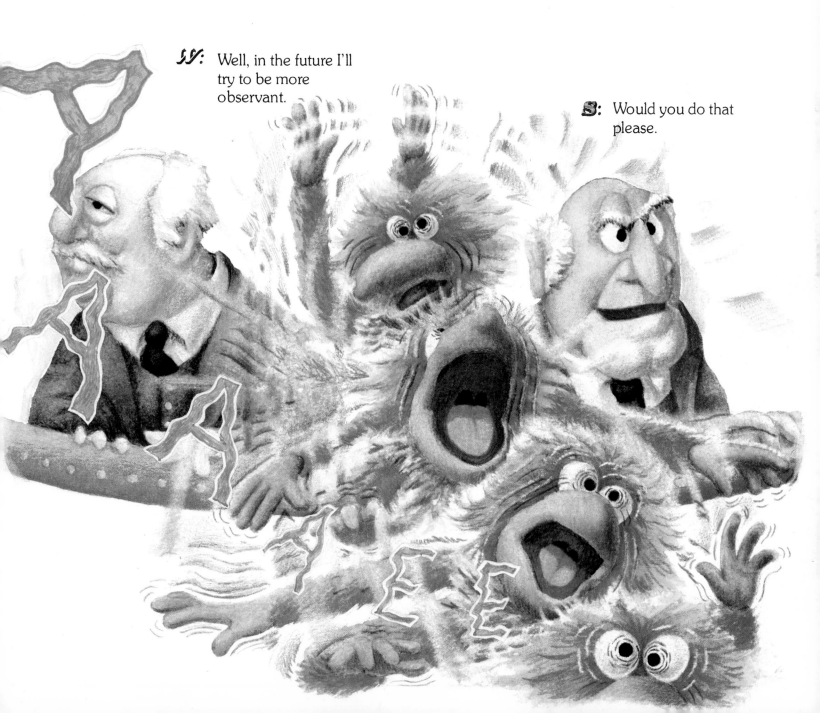

FOZZIE'S SHADES

FOZZIE BEAR

Ah, this is fun. Hey, I really want to thank you for letting me help plan tonight's show, Kermit.

Kermit

Yeah, well . . .

FLOYD

O.K., green thing, the band has asked me to have a word with you.

K: Yeah?

F: Yeah. I refer specifically to the closing number.

K: Oh boy.

K: Er, well, now . . . now I tell you. This is not my fault this time, see, because Fozzie Bear helped me plan tonight's show and *he* was the one that wanted the band to play "Lullaby of Birdland."

F: So it's the *bear's* doing, huh?

K: You bet!

𝄢: Oh, hi Floyd. Er, er, isn't, er, "Lullaby of Birdland" all right?

𝄠: All right? Hey, it's terrific!

𝄢: It *is*?

𝄦: It is???

𝄠: Yeah. "Lullaby of Birdland" is a jazz classic! At last we got some decent music in this gig.

𝄢: Ha!

𝄠: "Lullaby of Birdland"! Why isn't the *bear* running things around here?

𝄢: Yeah, why isn't the bear running things around here?

𝄦: Yeah! Why isn't the frog auditioning new comedians?

𝄢: Why isn't the bear keeping his mouth shut.

F: Fozzie, my main bear. Mmm, what it *is*! You know, everybody in the band is so blown away by the fact that you suggested we do "Lullaby of Birdland" on the show.

♪: Blown away??? Is that good?

F: Good?

♪: Yes.

F: Fozzie, you're so hip you make us flip. In fact, we just took a vote, and made you a bona fide, registered Hip Dude! You have won your shades.

♪: My shades?

F: Yeah, now, these are the official Charlie-Parker-Lives super-cool sunglasses.

♪: Oh! Thank you!

F: Welcome to Grooveydom.

♪: Oh. Oh, will you please tell the band how honored I am. Oh boy, I can't wait to tell Kermit.

KERMIT!

T
H
U
M
P
!.!

F: Hey, Fozzie, my main fuzzie.

ʄ: Who?

ʄ: Oh, Floyd.

F: Yeah . . . listen. You know, one of the dudes in the band is so turned on . . .

ʄ: Yeah?

F: . . . by the fact that you suggested we do "Lullaby of Birdland" . . .

ʄ: Yeah?

F: . . . he'd like to shake your hand personally.

ʄ: Hey, outa sight! O.K.

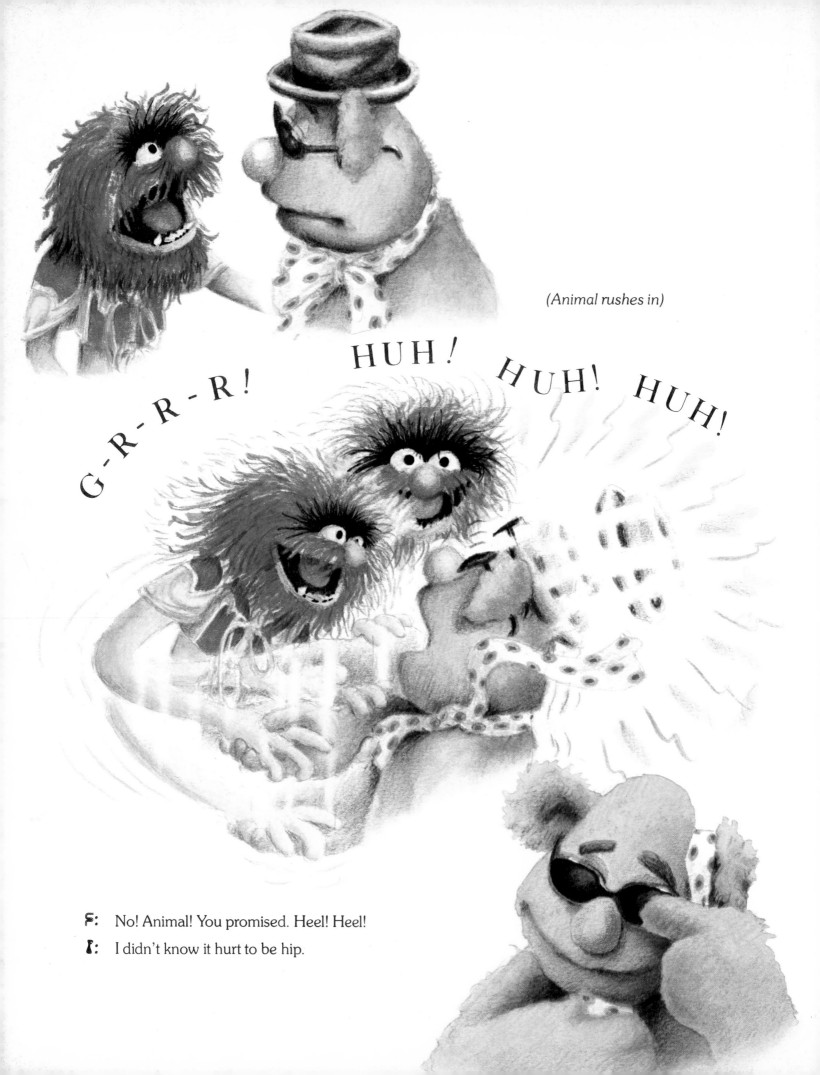

(Animal rushes in)

G-R-R-R! HUH! HUH! HUH!

F: No! Animal! You promised. Heel! Heel!

8:   I didn't know it hurt to be hip.

THE ORIGINAL KOOZEBANE SKETCH

This is Kermit the Frog speaking to you from the planet Koozebane. There is a hush in the air. This is the traditional time of courtship of the Koozebanian creatures. We are waiting now for the male Koozebanian creature to make the first move.

peep

peep peep peep

peep

Well, there you have it,
friends. The life cycle of
the Koozebanians!

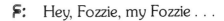

F: Hey, Fozzie, my Fozzie . . .

F: Hey!

F: Hey! Everything is everything . . .

F: Whatever!

F: Yeh . . . I was just wonderin' how you were enjoyin' your new title as official Hip Dude.

F: Oh, I love, it, I love it: Just wish it came with a flashlight.

(Kermit comes in)

K: It's time to do "Lullaby of Birdland."

F: Oh, yes, speaking of which . . . since I am playing vibes in this number we're going to need another player for the bass.

K: How can I find another bass player now? You're on.

F: Hey, Kermit, Kermit . . . no problem. I have already found the perfect bass player. Floyd, you just go out there and start cooking, baby.
(Continuing)
Yess, all right . . . and I will introduce this number for my hip brothers.

Hey, all right, all you hip dudes and swinging sisters out there . . . Oops!

Hey . . . all right, all you hip dudes and swinging sisters out there. Now a golden goodie from Fozzie's wiggy wonderland . . . the "Lullaby of Birdland!"

F: Hey, hey . . . me and the band just took another vote on accounta what happened in the Birdland number. You have been officially and permanently de-shaded.

S: Oh, NO! And just when I was getting used to working in the dark.

H♥WT♥ MAKE A FR♥G JEAL♥US!

MP: Scooter, Scooter . . . oh, dear nephew of the theater owner ? . . .

S: Well yes, Miss Piggy?

MP: Would you do Miss Piggy a favor?

S: Oh sure . . . why not.

MP: Mmm. Well, you may have noticed I have given my love to Kermit. You may also have noticed his reluctance in returning same.

S: Oh . . . so you want me to get your love from Kermit and give it back to you? Oh, O.K. Where does he keep it?

MP: Amusing little twit, isn't he? No, bonehead, I want you to make him jealous . . .

S: Oh . . . I see.

MP: I want you to tell him that this week's guest star is simply mad about me.

S: Oh, you want me to lie.

MP: Just do it.

S: And if I refuse?

MP: Well then I will karate chop you until the only thing you'll be able to go-fer . . . is down fer the count!

S: Er, one jealous frog, coming up.

K: Er, Scooter, would you go-fer our guest star and tell him to stand by for his next number?

S: Boss, you know there's nothing I wouldn't do for you.

K: Well, so far that's what you've done . . . nothing.

S: I would climb the highest mountain! I would swim the widest river! I'd walk across burning coals . . .

K: Please! Just go get our guest.

S: That I can't do.

K: WHAT??

S: Sorry, Boss, but he and Miss Piggy are in his dressing room and he told me he did not want to be disturbed.

K: Piggy and our guest star? Are you nuts? Why, he wouldn't touch her with a ten-foot pole.

S: You're right. He was touching her with his hands and also whispering sweet nothings into her ear . . . nothings like . . .

whisper whisper whisper

K: WILL YOU GET OUT OF HERE!!! Anybody want to buy a go-fer, cheap?

MP: Kermit, my love, my life . . . I am sorry if our guest star made you jealous . . . You *are* jealous aren't you?

K: Er, no . . . I'm not.
ER, FOZZIE BEAR, STAND BY!

MP: But why?

K: Well . . . Scooter told me it was all a trick.

S: ER, FOZZIE, STAND BY!

MP: SCOOTER! STAND BY!!!

W U M P H

K: Nice . . . ah . . . nice punch.

Who needs ya? FLIPPER FACE!

Er, do you believe in the hereafter?

Oh, yes.

Then you know what I'm hereafter.

My what big teeth you have.

I'm a conductor.

Oh, do you use them to punch holes in tickets?

No, in the musicians.

You know, my doctor says I'm getting the Asian flu.

What did he say to do?

He says take two fortune cookies and he'll call me in the morning.

Mmmm . . .
you're such a
smooth dancer.
Ever since we've
started I feel like
my feet have
never touched
the floor.

They haven't . . .
you've been
standing on
mine.

You know, my
marriage was
wrecked by
something really
stupid.

What was that?

My husband.

Do you prefer
Shakespeare to
Bacon?

I prefer anything
to bacon.

Lady
WRESTLERS

FLOYD: Hey, frogis amphibious, hey, don't forget today is . . . Payday!

Animal: Ahh! Payday! Payday!

Kermit: Payday? Again? It was payday last year. Seems to be getting a habit. Well, I'll see what's in the old cashbox here . . .

K: Three moths and a washer. Well, that's more than we usually have.

K: Oh, where am I going to get the payroll money?

Scooter: Oh, how much do you need, Kermit?

K: Oh, Scooter . . . twenty-seven dollars and fourteen cents.

S: Wow! That's high finance.

S: I'll get it. Hello? Oh, hi, Uncle J.P.

K: That's Scooter's uncle, J.P. Grosse, the bloodless old tightwad who owns this theater.

S: Yeah, yeah, well, listen . . . er, could you put your cigar out, please? Thanks. Everything's fine. Except, er, Kermit needs some money to make the payroll. Uh-huh . . . Uh-huh . . . Uh-huh . . . Uh-huh.

K: Well, what'd he say?

S: He said, "Uh-huh."

K: Terrific!

S: If . . .

K: If what?

S: If you put some good old-fashioned entertainment back into the show.

K: Oh, yeah . . . You mean like an Irish tenor?

S: No.

K: Er, a dog act? Jugglers? Spoon players? What?

S: Lady wrestlers.

K: Terrific . . . Lady wrestlers. I was afraid he wanted something tasteless.

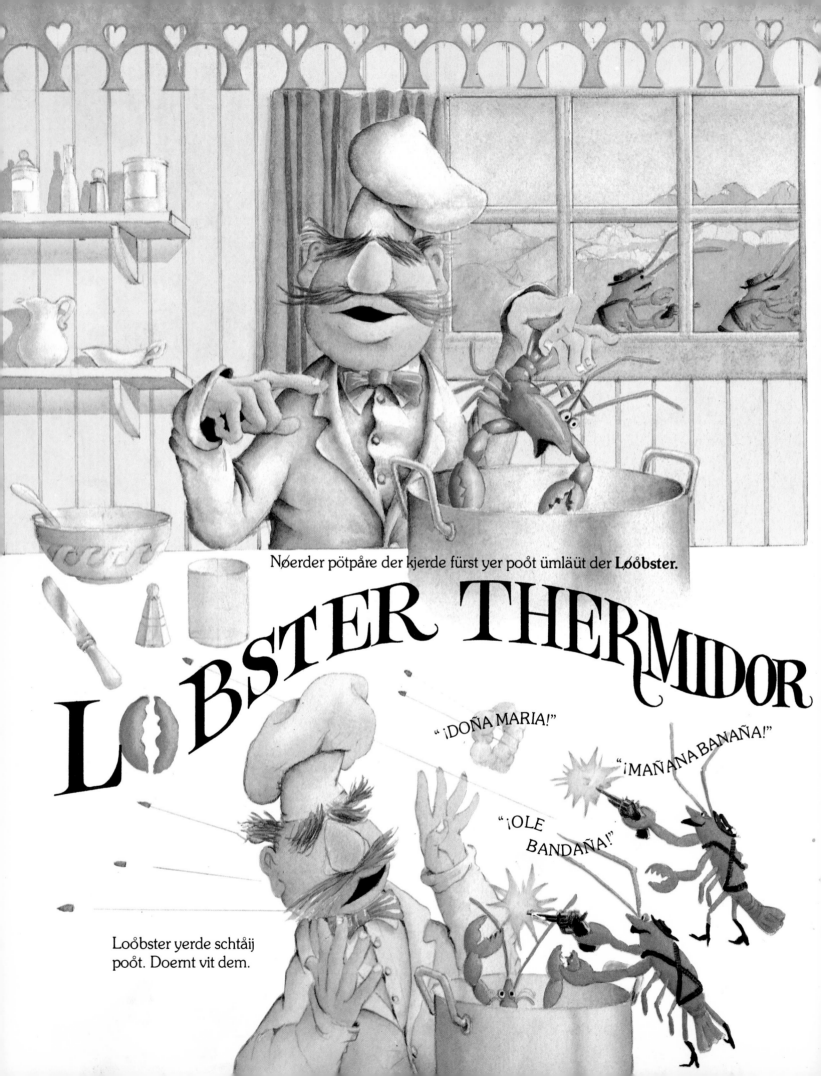

Er, where am I going to find a couple of lady wrestlers at this late date? Hello, Killer Katy, the Terror of Toledo? How'd you like to work The Muppet Show tonight? . . . I see, transcendental meditation. Well, that's too bad.

K: I'm sorry to keep you waiting, Ma'am. What can I, ah, do for you?

Granny: Yes, um, I understand you're looking for lady wrestlers. See, I'm Granny the Gouger, and I'd like to audition.

K: Ho hoo hohohoh. You want to audition? That's very funny! Is this some kind of a joke or something?

G: Joke? Funny? Young man, it's not nice to make fun of old ladies. You're going to be old yourself someday. And when that day comes, you are going to be sorry you were mean to Granny.

I think I am sorry already.

K: Look at that. The show's almost over, and I still haven't found another lady wrestler. Oh, where in the world am I going to find another heavyweight, aggressive, tough female with a killer's instinct?

MP: Hello, Kermie.

K: Oh, oh, hi, Miss Piggy!

MP: And pray tell, what is my wonderfulness doing?

K: Well, you see, I was just thinking that you'd be perfect for a special spot in tonight's show.

MP: Ah, you have created a spot just for *moi?* Oh, tell me about it, my little green ball of passion.

K: Er . . .

MP: Yes, yes? . . .

K: Ah, well, you see, this spot requires an actress with tremendous strength.

MP: Yes . . .

K: Er, versatility.

MP: Yes . . .

K: Er, and someone who's *all* female.

MP: What is it? Joan of Arc?

K: Er, no.

P: Naughty Marietta?

K: Well, no.

MP: Oh, Lady Macbeth.

K: Well, er . . . it, it's more like a lady wrestler.

MP: (Very reasonably) Lady wrestler?

K: Well, yeah, it, it's the sort of thing where, ah . . . you have to have the ability to . . . er . . . wrestle.

MP: LADY WRESTLER!!!

FLOYD: What d'you make of that, man?

ZOOT: Ten to one on the pig.

Tonight we're going to present you with a cultural demonstration of female grace and dexterity. So here they are, direct from the Bali Hai Bowl-a-drome . . . Granny the Gouger and the mysterious Ms. Mask! One fall, no holds barred!

STATLER
I think you'd better give up, frog!

K: What? And leave show business!

MP: What did you do to my frog!

G: Hmmm?

MP: I'll show you . . .

HIIIIII YAAAAA . . .

The Lives and Loves of Gonzo the Great: I

And now the band is playing very slow
And once again I'll get my coat and go
A lonely wallflower waiting by the wall
Without the willpower to face the music at all

Please, won't somebody dance with me
Start up a romance with me
Just someone to care, someone somewhere
Who will dance with me . . .

GONZO: Excuse me, it's, it's time to change partners.

Miss Piggy: No, it's time to change ballrooms, creep.

G: Excuse me, can I cut in?

Girl: That reminds me, Marvin, did you remember to feed the anteater?

G: *Please, won't somebody dance with me*
Start up a romance with me . . .

G: Oh, there she is!!! *(Gonzo rushes to chicken and they dance and romance.)*

Heaven! I'm in heaven...

FOZZIE: Oh Gonzo, I don't think very much of this summer cottage y-you rented for us.

GONZO: Yeah. I don't understand it. The ad looked so good in the paper.

F: What paper was that?

G: *The Wampire Veekly.*

F: *The Wampire Veekly?*

G: It does look kinda big for just the two of us.

(A ghost appears)

G: The three of us . . .

(Another ghost appears)

G: . . . er, four of us.

F: *(Terrified)* Well, at least we won't be lonely.
(KNOCK KNOCK)

G&F: AAAHH! Help!

F: S-someone's . . . someone's at the door. Someone's at the door!

G: I bet it's not the Welcome Wagon.

(Fozzie opens door. Vincent Price enters in cape looking his most ominous.)

F: Yup. It's not the Welcome Wagon.

VP: Good evening. Excuse me, but do you have a room for the night? You see, the road has washed out and my horse has a flat tire.

F: Er, well, yeah, well, maybe, I, I, I . . .

VP: I must tell you, I am not alone. I am traveling with my beautiful assistant and a hideously deformed monster.

Uncle Deadly: Watch it. I'm the beautiful assistant.

G: Oh, boy.

UD: Master . . .

UP: Mmm?

UD: I've left Hulko in the coach.

ʃ: Hulko!

UP: Oh, good, good. (Laughs) And now I must ask . . . can you tell me what time it is?

ʃ: Er . . . oh golly, my hour glass seems to have stopped.

UP: This is terrible.

ʃ: Why is that?

UD: Because every night at the stroke of midnight the master turns into a screaming, maniacal, demonic, raging, blood-lusting animal!

UP: And then I get mean. Quickly, quickly! Prepare a dungeon—chains, manacles, bind me . . . "Bong" . . . Argh!!! . . . "Bong" Oh, no. "Bong" It's too late, "Bong" something's different. "Bong" Oh, quick, what night is it? "Bong"

G: New Year's Eve! "Bong"

UD: Oh, no, "Bong" this is too cruel, "Bong" too inhuman! "Bong"

ʃ: What, what, what is? "Bong" What, tell, tell, what, what! "Bong"

On New Year's Eve, the master turns into Guy Lombardo!

And now an act you're going to get a big charge out of! The ...

CRAZY HARRY: Did you say a big charge?

HA! HA! HA! HA! HA! HA!

GONZO: Uh . . . Kermit . . . are you busy?

Kermit: Er, yes, Gonzo . . . but I can give you my ear for a moment.

G: What would I do with your ear?

K: Van Gogh impressions.

WHY DO YOU HAVE TO TAKE EVERYTHING SO LITERALLY?
That's just an expression.

GONZO: Kermit, what I wanted to know was, was er . . . you know . . . I've noticed that I haven't been on, er, on stage for the last couple of shows.

K: Good observation.

G: Yeah, well, er, Kermit . . . I have a lot of fans out there, see, who are waiting to see my latest theatrical creation.

K: Er, Gonzo, I have seen you eat a rubber tire to music . . . and I have seen you play a concert on your head with a mallet . . .

G: Yeah.

K: . . . and Gonzo, my dear friend, it doesn't work.

G: Wha . . . Kermit, I don't—you gotta understand—I don't play for the masses! I'm an *artist*! You understand that? An *artist*!

K: Yeah? Well . . . then you should have gotten my Van Gogh joke. Listen, Gonzo, why don't you get yourself a manager, you know . . . somebody who could guide your career.

G: All right.
O.K. I will. All right I'll
do that and then you'll see . . .
You'll all *see* because
there's only one Great Gonzo!
Only one!

K: Thank goodness for
that.

ECOLOGY: AN OPINION BY SAM THE EAGLE

Greetings. As an American eagle, I feel it is my duty to say a few words about the glories of industry and technology. Yea, verily, today the very fiber of our industrialization is under attack from a small subversive group of namby-pamby conservationists. These weirdos would stop the march of progress for the sake of a few insignificant animals! I have here a list of the animals these so-called conservationists would have us protect. Just listen to this! The mountain lion. Huh! The alligator. Huh! the coyote, the timber wolf. Huh! The American bald eagle . . . the American bald eagle? . . . Excuse me, this list is now inoperative.

Scooter: Hey, hey Kermit . . . the Great Gonzo wants me to manage him.

GONZO: Yeah, Scooter understands the soul of a true artist.

S: Mmm.

Kermit: Er, yeah, but Scooter . . . I hired you as a go-fer . . . go-fer coffee . . . go-fer sandwiches . . . remember?

S: Yeah, well I can still do that . . . but Gonzo needs personal management.

G: Oh I do, Kermit. I truly do.

S: Yeah, I'm gonna change his whole repertoiree . . . I'm gonna have him do a rock act.

K: A rock act. But Gonzo can't sing!

S: No, no. I mean a *rock* act. Show him Gonzo.

G: Watch.

S: O.K. Hit it, kid.

ART! ART! ART!

OUT! OUT! OUT!

DR. BUNSEN HONEYDEW

Welcome again to Muppetlab where the future is being made today. And here it is folks, the product you've all been waiting for . . . the new solid-state gorilla detector.

How many times have you awakened at night in the dark and said to yourself, "Is there a gorilla in here?" Whenever a gorilla comes anywhere *near* this device its lights will flash and its bell will ring.

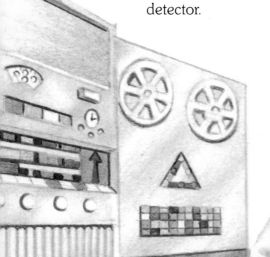

Think of the safety! Think of the sense of well-being! At last your family can be protected from the heartbreak of gorilla invasion.

Err . . . that creature is *not* a gorilla. If he *were* a gorilla the lights would flash and the bell would ring.

Yes, Muppet technology is wonderful. It tells us that we are not seeing a gorilla smash the cabinet.

So I know scientifically that I am not being eaten by a gorilla . . . ARGH!

Hilda: Kermit, Kermit . . . that nephew of the theater owner . . .

K: Scooter? What about him?

H: He is going to drive me bananas. He has gone all through the wardrobe. He wants the Great Gonzo to do a costume act.

S: Hey, chief, what d'ya think?

G: D'you think the high heels are too much?

K: ARE YOU GUYS NUTS???

G: Well, Scooter says that female impersonation is a noble art.

K: Of all the dumb acts that Gonzo has come up with, this is the dumbest.

S: Well, gee, my uncle loves it.

K: You go on right after the dancers.

G: But what do I do when I get out there?

K: Duck!

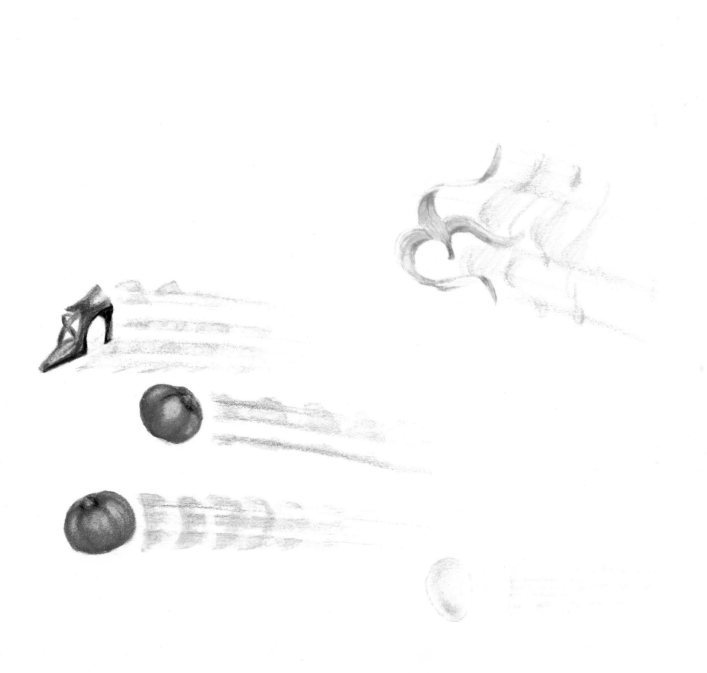

Miss Piggy "Buys the House"

Scooter

Boy! They really love her, don't they?

Kermit

Yeah, must be an easy house.

Miss Piggy

(Backing in from stage):
Ah, ah. Oh, no, no, please!
Oh, you're too kind. Kissy, kissy!

(Kermit exits)

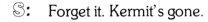

S: Forget it. Kermit's gone.

MP: Oh. Did it work?

S: Nope. But how about that audience I paid off for you, huh? They did just what I told them to . . . go hog wild.

MP: Scooter, I'm paying you to give me help . . . not for cheap jokes. Ah, Scooter, ah, Scooter my dear impressionable young lad. You must understand that I am only doing this in order to make the frog notice me more.

S: Sure, and if you happen to get your own spot on the show, well, that wouldn't hurt!

MP: Your life's hangin' on a thread, kid . . .

S: Yes, ma'am. I'll go write some more spontaneous sincere fan mail for you.

Hmmm. Ah yes, you know the words:
gorgeous . . . beautiful . . . modest . . .

Vit der vun und tu scjpøóns,
yu måk spógättü märónäru.

Tïngle tånglé spógättü.

Såücy märónäru güd!

SLURP   SLURP

Sjtay spógättü on der dishy dishy

S: Gee, Miss Piggy. What are you going to do?

(Kermit, of course, stops and listens)

MP: I have . . . I just don't know, Scooter. My loyalty is, of course, to Kermit. But this other show has offered me a contract at twice the money.

S: Well, you *are* a superstar.

MP: Ahhhhhh. No, I'm not!

S: Uh…

MP: *(Whispers)* Yes, you are!

S: Yes, you are.

MP: Well, I shall just have to think about it.
(exits)

(Kermit enters, upstairs)

K: Scooter, that act that you and Miss Piggy put on for me was terrible.

S: Gee, I didn't think it was that bad. I missed one line but . . . oh, no . . .

K: Scooter, are you going to tell me what's going on?

S: No, I promised.

K: I'll give you a raise.

S: *(Quickly)* Well, the flowers are fake, the audience was paid off, I wrote the fan letters, and Miss Piggy doesn't have another offer.

K: Scooter, I like your style!

MP: Kermie, Kermie, ah . . . you wanted to see me?

K: Uh, yes, Miss Piggy. You know, I couldn't help but overhear that conversation between you and Scooter . . . about that offer you got from that other show . . .

MP: Oh, Kermie . . . I am *so sorry!* I didn't want you to hear that . . . Oh, that terrible boy!

K: Ah yeah, well . . . Actually, I'm kinda glad that I did because I have come to a decision that I think will make you very happy.

MP: Oh?

K: I've decided to let you go.

MP: You've WHAT???

K: You see, Piggy, I don't want to stand in your way.

MP: But, but Kermie . . . I . . .

K: Good luck, kid,

MP: Um . . . well, er . . . I'll just go clear out my dressing room, then.

K: That would be very nice. Thank you.

MP: Um . . . you'll . . . you'll explain to everyone what happened, Kermie?

K: Oh, sure. (quietly) What a ham!

MP: Kermie . . . I can't leave you . . . I can't leave you . . . I can't.

K: Well, er . . . does this mean you want your job back? Yes? Oh, good. Er . . . but incidentally . . . though . . . you will have to take a pay cut.

MP: WHAT?

K: Well, sure, I mean, you know if you can afford to pay off the audience and buy all those flowers and furs and the mail and all that stuff, then I think you can . . . ah . . . ah . . .

MP: You knew all the time!

A A A A A A A A A A A!

The Lives and Loves of Gonzo the Great: II

Kermit: I don't know how the cow got in here. Usually, we're much more careful about who we allow in this place.

GONZO: Yeah, I can see that.

K: Er, it's been a bad night for security.

G: *(To cow)* Wow, you gotta great pair of legs. In fact, she's got two great pair of legs. Hey, er, you wouldn't think about going into show business would you? Will you at least have dinner with me … promise?

UP UP AND AWAY!

Golly, it went!

FOZZIE: Where is that handsome frog? Oh, there you are, old frog friend.

Kermit: What?

F: Would you lend me a fiver till payday?

K: Fozzie, you already owe me five.

F: Oh, please, please, I know it, but I got to pay my writer, the legendary "Gags" Beasley.

K: The legendary "Gags" comes pretty cheap, doesn't he?

F: Well, er, we worked out a good deal.

K: Ah, you pay him by the line?

F: No, I pay him by the laugh.

K: Oh . . . then he owes *you* money.

BANANA SKETCH

Oh, that was cute, that was real cute, frog!

F: Ahh, thank you, thank you, thank you. Look out, I've got some great ones for you tonight . . . aahhhhh . . . oh, I'm rolling now . . . I'm on a roll . . . I'm on a roll . . .

WALDORF

Yeah, well why don't you butter yourself and slip on out of here.

F: Speaking of slipping, are you guys familiar with the banana sketch?

STATLER

Oh, nice transition.

W: Smooth.

S: Good blend.

Hey, hey, these two bananas are walking down the street . . .

(Enter Hilda)

K: Well, he's got a new writer– "Gags" Beasley.

S: Not the legendary "Gags" Beasley.

K: You mean you've heard of him?

S: Well, who hasn't?

K: Me, for one.

S: Oh.

Hilda : But "Gags" Beasley, he is to comedy what Mozart was to music. He wrote the famous banana sketch.

K: The banana sketch . . . what's the banana sketch?

H: You never heard of the banana sketch? But it's the funniest . . .

(Fozzie returns from stage)

F: Ahh, ahh, ahh, hear that?

K: Great, great.

F: Oh boy, I killed 'em. Oh boy. Yeah, I closed with the banana sketch, you know.

K: Fozzie, what is the banana sketch???

F: You never heard of the banana sketch? Hey guys, Kermit never heard of the banana sketch!

K: I think somebody's pulling my leg . . . Somebody *is* pulling my leg. It's the Great Gonzo.

G: You never heard of the banana sketch?

WILL YOU CUT THAT OUT!

BEIN'

GREEN

It's not easy Bein' Green
having to spend each day
the color of leaves . . .

When I think it might be nicer
being red, or yellow or gold
or something much more colorful like that

It's not easy
Bein' Green
seems you blend in with so many
other ordinary things
and people tend to pass you over
'cause you're not standing out
like flashy sparkles in the water
or stars in the sky.

But green's the color of Spring
and green can be cool and friendly-like
and green can be big like a mountain
or important like a river
or tall like a tree.

When green is all there is to be
it could make you wonder why
but why wonder
why wonder
I am green and
it'll do fine
(it's beautiful)
and I think it's what I want to be.

MP: Oh, frog of my life, please tell me what they're saying about you is not true.

K: What's that, Piggy?

MP: Well, that you . . . you . . . host of a television show, veteran of the boards . . . you have never heard of the banana sketch.

K: Er, Piggy, said the frog trying to refrain from losing his cool and looking like a bad sport, there is no banana sketch, there never was a banana sketch, and there never will be a banana sketch!!!

MP: Hmm, touchy, touchy.

BANANA

Hey, which way to my dressing room? And don't try to shove me into the refrigerator.

Scooter: Hey boss . . . Muppy and I wanted to talk to you about the act we're doing on the show tonight.

Kermit: Er, Scooter, you're not doing an act on the show tonight.

S: Oh gee, my uncle–who–owns–this–theater thought of this act.

K: Did he? Um, er, tell us about the act you're doing on the show tonight.

S: Oh, it's called Simon Smith and His Amazing Dancing Dog. Yeah, I sing this song, see, and Muppy here does this cute, adorable, sweet, sugary little dance.

K: Er, well it sounds—says the frog displaying his artistic judgment—sappy.

S: Gee, my uncle thought . . .

K: Er, it sounds—says the frog, displaying his will to survive—*wonderful!*

S: Yeah, it's great. You'll love it.

K: Um, certainly. I've often thought of Muppy here as about the cutest little fellow around.

GGRRRRR

SSSSS

(Exit Kermit—hastily)

Animal

K: I, er, thought some of you might like to know a little bit more about, er, our drummer, who we affectionately refer to as Animal.

A: A-ni-mal!

K: That's his name, actually. Animal, why don't you tell our audience how long have you been playing the drums?

A: Ah, er . . . *(bangs his head on drums five times)*

K: One . . . two . . . three . . . four . . . five.

        A: Aah!

        K: Five years.

        A: Aah!

K: Yes, O.K., well I guess your drums mean a great deal to you, eh?

A: Aah yeah. —Oh nice!

K: Yeah, er, listen. —I imagine you have a lot of idols.

A: Yeah!

K: Buddy Rich . . .

A: Oh, yeah, yeah!

K: Gene Krupa . . .

A: Yeah . . . Krupa, Krupa!

K: Tony Chequers . . .

A: Ton—What?

K: He's our new drummer. He begins next week.

K: Then again . . . maybe not.

S: Hey, Kermit, Muppy wants you to know he's very sorry he bit you.

K: Oh yeah?

S: He wants you to know he's very grateful you're letting him do the Simon Smith number.

K: Oh, that's nice.

S: He wants you to know he wants his own dressing room and star billing.

K: What? Who is this crazy dog?

S: My uncle's favorite pet.

SLURRP!

EECCHH!

S: Hey, hey, Kermit . . .?

K: Mm?

S: Yeah, now that Muppy is doing the big Simon Smith number, well, he only has one other suggestion.

K: Listen, I already gave him his own dressing room. What more does he want?

S: Well, it's about the title of the show. Er, look . . .

K: THE MUPPY SHOW???!!

E E E F A A A A A G H!!

Muppy, Scooter . . . you're on next.

S: Oh, it's no use, Kermit. Muppy says if you won't change the title of the show, he's not going on. He's locked himself in his dressing room and he's not coming out.

K: Yeah, but, but, that Simon Smith number is on next! What're we gonna do?
(Fozzie enters)

ƒ: Kermit, K,-Kermit, Kermit . . . how come I'm not doing an act this week? Mm?

K: Er, ah, congratulations, Fozzie, you're doing an act this week.

Sometimes I can be very persuasive.

The Lives and Loves of Gonzo the Great: III

And now the band is playing very slow
And once again I'll get my coat and go
A lonely wallflower waiting by the wall
Without the willpower to face the music at all

MP: "My dearest Piggy, you must know how much I love you, I cannot pretend any longer. I will wait for you in the dressing room, *mon cher.*"

Oh, it has happened! Oh, my Kermit has admitted his love for me at last. And now he awaits within. Oh, come to my arms, my passionflower.

(Miss Piggy opens the door)

MP: I am here, my love.

T H W A C K !

G: She kissed me . . .
She put her arms around me
And she kissed me.

MP: It was a case of mistaken identity!

G: Oh, *hug* me, Miss Piggy. *Hold* me.

MP: I will *not* hug you, you twit-turkey!

G: Oh, hold my hand,
pig-of-my-dreams!

MP: Will you beat it, twerp.

G: Just touch me, o hog-of-my-heart!

MP: Here's a touch for you,
wimp-buzzard!

G: I'm ready!

W H U M P H !

GONZO: Excuse me, Miss Piggy. May I come in?

Miss Piggy: Only if you're green and have flippers.

G: It's me, Gonzo. And it'll only take a second.

MP: O.K., twerp, what do you want?

G: Well, you know I've always had this crush on you.

MP: Yuck!

G: I came to tell you I'm not going to bother you any more.
I'm sorry.

MP: Well good, I'm glad you've finally come to your senses.
Ohh, my dear Gonzo, I know it will be painful for a while,
but in time you shall forget all about me.

G: But, I already have.

MP: OH???

G: Yes, I've found somebody else.

MP: Well. Er, you have? What . . .
er, hmm . . . what's she like?

G: Well, she's nothing like you at all.

MP: Mmmm.

G: She's beautiful, and, and, she's got the cutest little nose, and she's intelligent, and talented . . . and I'm very happy. So you see, breaking up with you isn't painful at all.

MP: N-O-T   U-N-T-I-L   N-O-W!

I see what you mean . . .

(The setting is an art class,
Candice Bergen is the model.
Andre is the teacher, all the
others are students painting her
picture.)

Andre: Look at that face
Just look at it,
Look at that fabulous
Face of yours.
I knew first look
I took at it,
This was a face
That the world adores.

Look at those eyes
As wise and as deep
As the sea,
Look at that nose
It shows what a nose
Should be.

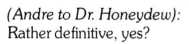

(Andre to Dr. Honeydew):
Rather definitive, yes?

(Andre to Mildred):
Inspired, but by what?

(Andre to Miss Piggy): Mm . . . interesting.

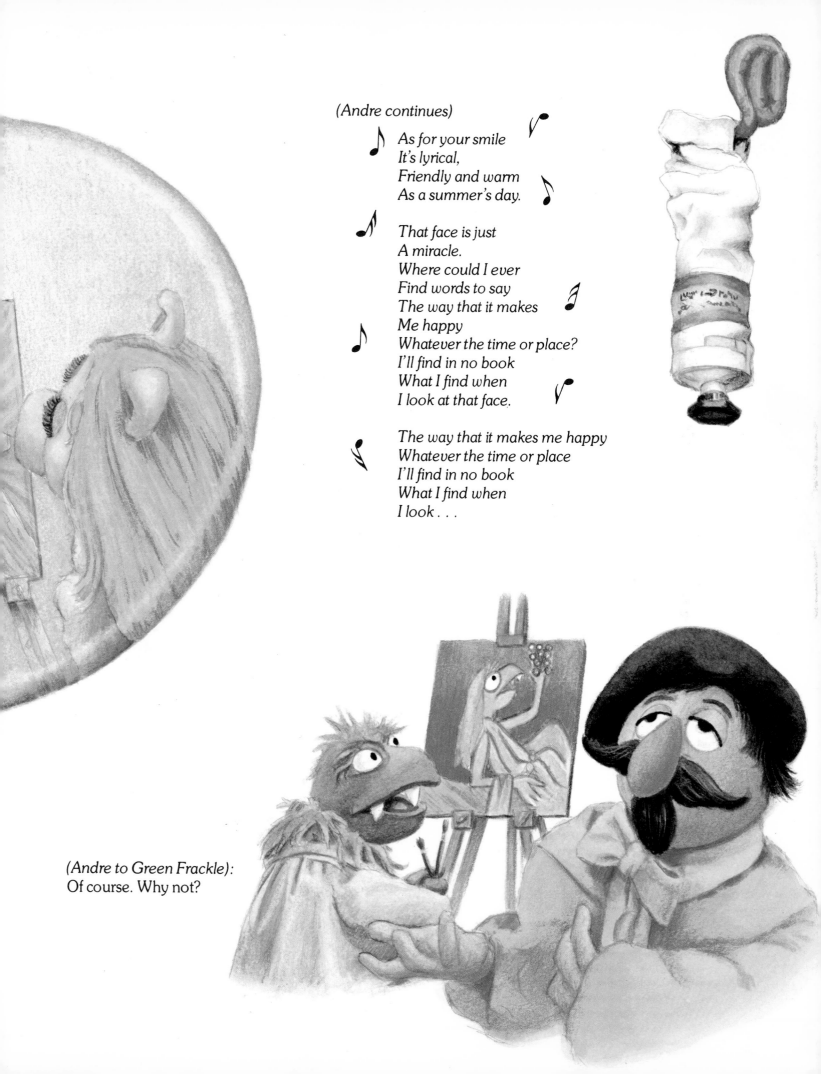

(Andre continues)

♪ *As for your smile*
It's lyrical,
Friendly and warm
As a summer's day.

♪ *That face is just*
A miracle.
Where could I ever
Find words to say
The way that it makes
Me happy
Whatever the time or place?
I'll find in no book
What I find when
I look at that face.

♪ *The way that it makes me happy*
Whatever the time or place
I'll find in no book
What I find when
I look . . .

(Andre to Green Frackle):
Of course. Why not?

A: Animal, that does not look like her. I told you to paint her!

A: Oh, thank you.

A: *What I find when*
I look at that face.

THE KOOZEBANE PHOOBS

This is Kermit the Frog speaking to you from the planet Koosebane, and today I am interviewing a most unfortunate creature-the Koosebanian Phoob.

P: Thank you, thank you. I'm pleased to be here. As a matter of fact, I'm pleased to be anywhere.

K: I—I can believe that. Because, you see, folks, the Phoob is known as the most delicious creature on Koosebane.

P: That's true. We have a saying on this planet: "I never met a Phoob I didn't like—especially with mushroom gravy."

K: I suppose this tends to hold down the Phoob population pretty effectively.

P: Not really. Actually my species is flourishing.

K: Oh, really? How do you manage that?

P: Evolution.

K: I—I don't think I understand.

P: We Phoobs tend to evolve rather faster than most creatures.

K: Hm, hm . . . Well, what do you evolve *into?*

P: Oh, you know. Whatever's handy.

K: I . . . I beg your pardon?

P: We try to blend in with the crowd as best we can.

K: Say . . . are, are you changing?

P: Evolving. Evolving is the accurate term.

K: Yeah, but . . . you're starting to look familiar.

P: I should certainly hope so.

K: This . . . this is very weird. Good grief. Even your clothes are the same!

P: *(In Kermit's voice)* It's called the survival of the trench-coated.

K: Yeah, but you can't do this!

P: Ah, this is Kermit the Frog, returning you to . . .

K: I'm Kermit the Frog!   P: I am!   K: I am!

K & P: *(together)* Er, these are Kermit the Frogs, returning you to the Muppet Show.

Culture at Last

Kermit: Boy, Sam really has this place looking good for Rudolf Nureyev.

Scooter: Yeah, well, I don't mind that so much. But me 'n' Robin are mad we have to wear these formal clothes!

K: You and *Robin?* Where's Robin?

S: Oh, right here.

Robin: It's the only hat I could find.

(Scooter replaces the hat)

(Sam enters)

SAM: Attention!

K: Beg pardon?

S: Line up for inspection.

K: Inspection?

S: Yes, we must look proper for Mr. Nureyev. At last, to have a man of dignity, a man of culture on this weird, sick program.
(To Kermit) Did you wash your flippers?

K: Errr . . . yessir!

S: Let's have a look. Will you please get off the floor.

(To Scooter) Will you, will you comb your hair and polish those shoes.

S: Er, yes sir, yes sir.

S: And one more thing. Robin, your hat's too big!

K: Er, Sam, can I introduce the show now?

S: Of course, yes, But just do it with dignity!

K: Er, yes, yes.

S: Oh, to have the brilliant, talented Rudolf Nureyev on our show! He's my favorite opera singer!

K: Thank you, thank, you, thank you. Hi there and welcome to The Muppet Show!

S: You call *that* dignity?

K: I'm sorry, Sam . . . Er, ladies and gentlemen, it is indeed an honor . . .

S: Good.

K: . . .to welcome you to The Muppet Show. Er, tonight's guest star is one of the world's great masters of ballet, Mr. Rudolf Nureyev.

S: Well, wh—whe . . . are you sure it's ballet, not opera?

K: Positive.

S: Six of one, half-a-dozen of the other—culture is culture. Go ahead, go ahead.

K: Er, but here to get things started is Dr. Teeth and The Electric . . .

S: Not Dr. Teeth!

K: Sam, I know I've promised you a very cultural show. But don't worry. You see, they're playing a minuet, and they have promised to be very classy.

S: May I have that in writing?

(Band breaks into Mayhem number)

K: Not very cultural, guys. Not very cultural.

S: That was degrading! That was awful! Mr. Nureyev must be shocked!

K: Well, I doubt it.

S: Well, of course he is! He is sensitive, he is creative, he is artistic.

K: It's O.K. He is not here. He just phoned in. He's running a little bit late.

S: Oh, thank goodness. Now remember, when Mr. Nureyev arrives, we must be dignified, we must be respectful!

(The stage door opens. Rudolf Nureyev comes bounding up the stairs.)

RN: Hi, guys! I'm here!

S: Not for long you are not! We are waiting for Mr. Nureyev!

K: Sam!

S: (Continues) I'll handle this. Get out of here, you freak! You hippie! You weirdo! Get out! Move, move! Don't come back!

(Sam turns Rudolf around and gives him a push. Rudolf stumbles back down the steps and right out the door.)

S: Who do these punk kids think they are?

K: Th—that one thinks he's Rudolf Nureyev.

S: What!

K: In fact, that was Rudolf Nureyev.

S: What have I done?

S: Mr. Nureyev—will you ever forgive me?

(Kermit enters)

K: Er, he forgives you, Sam.

S: What?

K: I just talked to him. He isn't angry. He's putting on his costume for his big ballet number.

S: Oh, bless you frog. Oh, thank you for these glad tidings! And what ballet, may I ask, is the incomparable Mr. Nureyev going to perform?

K: Er, Swinelake.

S: Oh, good. Yes, culture. Dignity at last! SWINELAKE!!!

The Pigs Take Over

Kermit: Thank you, thank you, thank you, and welcome to The Muppet Show. Hey, you're going to love tonight's show because we have a very special guest. But first, first let's get things started . . .
Hey, what, what are you guys doing?

Pig I: We're taking over the show. —Yeah, taking over!

K: You'll never get away with it.

Pig II: Wanta bet?

Pig III: We did it. We did it. Ha! Ha!

Kermit the Pig: Hello, Kermit the Pig here. Hey, welcome to The Muppet Show. But tonight let's open the festivities with . . . *(Miss Piggy rushes in)*

MP: All right, buster! What's going on here? Where's my frog?

K: Oh, we pigs are taking over the show.

MP: Well, hoo-hah! Where's my frog, huh? What happened to him?

K: But Miss Piggy, *you* are starring in the opening number.

MP: I don't care. If you touch one flipper of my frog . . . I'M STARRING in the opening number???

K: Of course! You're the biggest pig star we've got!

MP: We'll talk about whatsisname later . . .

FOZZIE: Kermit, Kermit, now listen. Oh, Kermit, I'm so glad to see you. Oh, it's been terrible. Kermit, did you know that the pigs have taken over the show?

K: Er, where are we, is this the boiler room?

F: Yes, the boiler room.

K: Now listen, Fozzie, don't worry. We will get out of here.

F: OF COURSE we'll get out of here, because I, the bear, have a plan. I am going to tie some sheets together and we will slip out the window.

K: What window?

F: NO WINDOW? Oh Kermit, Kermit . . . we gotta bust out of here. K–Kermit, there's no telling how long they could keep us here.

K: Fozzie, Fozzie, Fozzie . . . do not panic.
Listen, we'll use that telephone there
and call for help.

The telephone! Of course! Hey, it's
working! Here, Kermit.

OOPS!!!

K: This may take longer than I thought.

(Inside boiler room Fozzie is standing by door holding a club poised for striking)

F: O.K., hey, Kermit. Now listen, when the pig comes in I'll clobber him, and then we run for our lives. Here we go . . .

GONZO: Owwwwww!!! Are you crazy? That really hurt!

F: Oh. Gonzo. I'm sorry. I thought you were a pig.

G: Terrific. Terrific. First he clobbers me, then he insults me.

K: Hey, er, Gonzo, what's happening with the show?

G: Oh, it's going great. They got this new M.C. and the audience loves him—Kermit the Pig.

K: Kermit the Pig!

F: Easy, easy, Kermit, don't take it so personally.

G: And the new comedian—Fozzie Pig. Boy, is he funny!

F: We *gotta* get out of here!

We will get out of here. Look what I smuggled in.

(He produces a spoon)

G: I'm going to dig a tunnel with it.

(He starts chipping away at huge wall)

K: Ah, I think this may take longer than we thought.

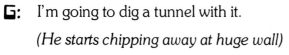

(Fozzie is at hole in the wall)

K: How's it going?

F: Oh, it's terrific! Gonzo's digging and I'm taking the dirt out.

(Miss Piggy enters in space costume)

MP: Kermie, oh, Kermie, are you all right?

K: Ah, well, er, er, yes, I guess so.

MP: Oh Kermie, I just want you to know that I have had nothing to do, whatsoever, with the taking over of this show. I have—no, really—I have refused to cooperate. Yes, and Kermie, I am going to stay here with you.

K: Oh, you, you really . . . oh, that's very nice of you.

MP: Oh, Kermie, my loyalty is here. With my frog.

K: You really mean that?

MP: Mmm-mm.

guard
"Pigs In Space" on next.

MP: You'll have to cancel it. I, I remain with my sweetheart, Kermie.

K: Ah, gee, Miss Piggy, you really shouldn't.

g: We'll get someone to take your place.

MP: TAKE MY PLACE??????

g: Well, if you want to stay here with him.

MP: Oh, Kermie, Kermie . . . I leave my heart with you . . . but NOBODY can TAKE MY PLACE! 'Bye!

g: Well, that's show biz.

PIGS IN SPACE

And now, "Pigs In Space"! Featuring the stout-hearted Captain Link Hogthrob, the fetching First Mate Miss Piggy, and the ubiquitous Dr. Julius Strangepork. Last week the spaceship Swinetrek was rapidly approaching the electrifying mid-course correction maneuver.

S: Stand by for mid-course correction.

MP: Oh, Isn't this electrifying!

L: Dr. Strangepork, ready to count me down?

MP: Oh, Captain Link, would it be all right if *I* performed the mid-course correction?

L: Well . . .

MP: After all, I *did* go to school for this particular maneuver for 11 years.

L: Still, you are a woman.

MP: Yes, Captain, just as you are a man.

S: Technically, you are both pigs, but we know what you're talking about.

L: Well, I suppose you can perform the maneuver, Piggy.

MP: Oh, thank you, Herr Capitain! Oh!

S: Twenty-five seconds to mid-course correction.

L: Don't forget which button to push.

MP: Ah, I know which button to push. I studied it for 11 years.

S: Fifteen seconds.

L: It's this button right here.

MP: I know it's that button!

S: Ten seconds.

L: Just push it when he tells you.

MP: I know, I know!

S: Five seconds.
(Dr. Strangepork counts down:) three, two, one.

L: Don't panic, First Mate Piggy.

MP: Will you shut up!

L: Don't tell me to shut up. I'm your Captain.

S: Now! Push the button! Push the button!

L: Push the button!

MP: I'm going to. Just don't shout at me — I'm a lady.

L: If you don't push that button, I'll push it myself.

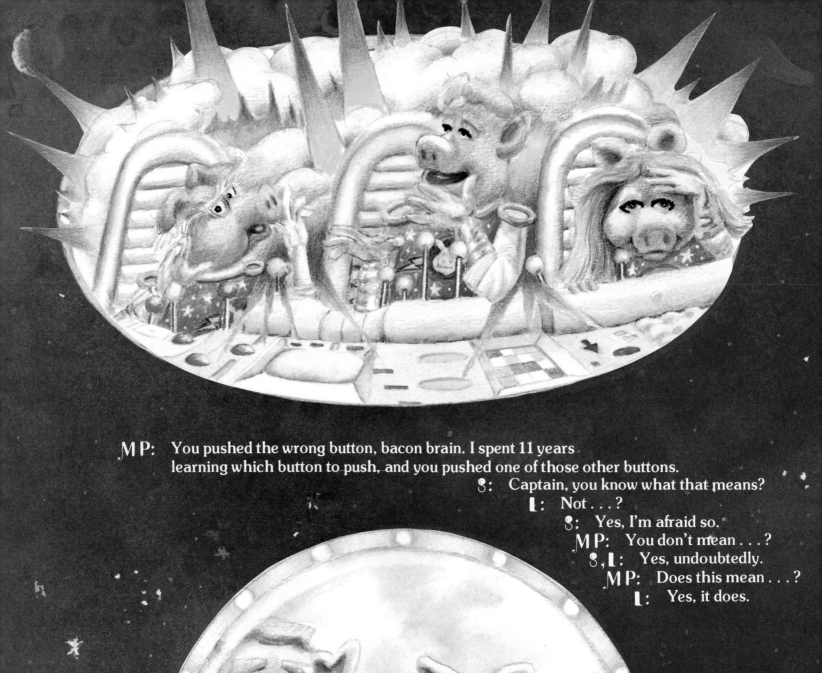

MP: You pushed the wrong button, bacon brain. I spent 11 years
learning which button to push, and you pushed one of those other buttons.

S: Captain, you know what that means?

L: Not . . . ?

S: Yes, I'm afraid so.

MP: You don't mean . . . ?

S, L: Yes, undoubtedly.

MP: Does this mean . . . ?

L: Yes, it does.

Tune in next week
and don't miss
the continuation
of "Pigs In Space"!

K: How's Gonzo doing?

🐀: Pretty good, I guess. I can't even see him anymore.

Scooter

Hey, Kermit! We're free, we're free! Someone next door started a hog calling contest so they all heard it and ran off!

🐀: What a plot twist! How amazing, how unbelievable.

K: How convenient! I'll get on stage, you tell Gonzo.

🐀: Hey Gonzo. Gonzo. Where are you? Boy, you've made a lot of progress with that teaspoon . . . Gonzo!

GONZO: Freedom is mine! Why, Kermit! What are you doing here? How did *you* get out?

K: I'm not sure, but someone started a hog calling contest . . .

G: Of course! Ingenious!

Here's a Muppet Newsflash!

Robin

Uncle Kermit, despite my small size and diminutive stature, I have learned to be the center of attraction, wherever I go, and I want a feature part in the show!

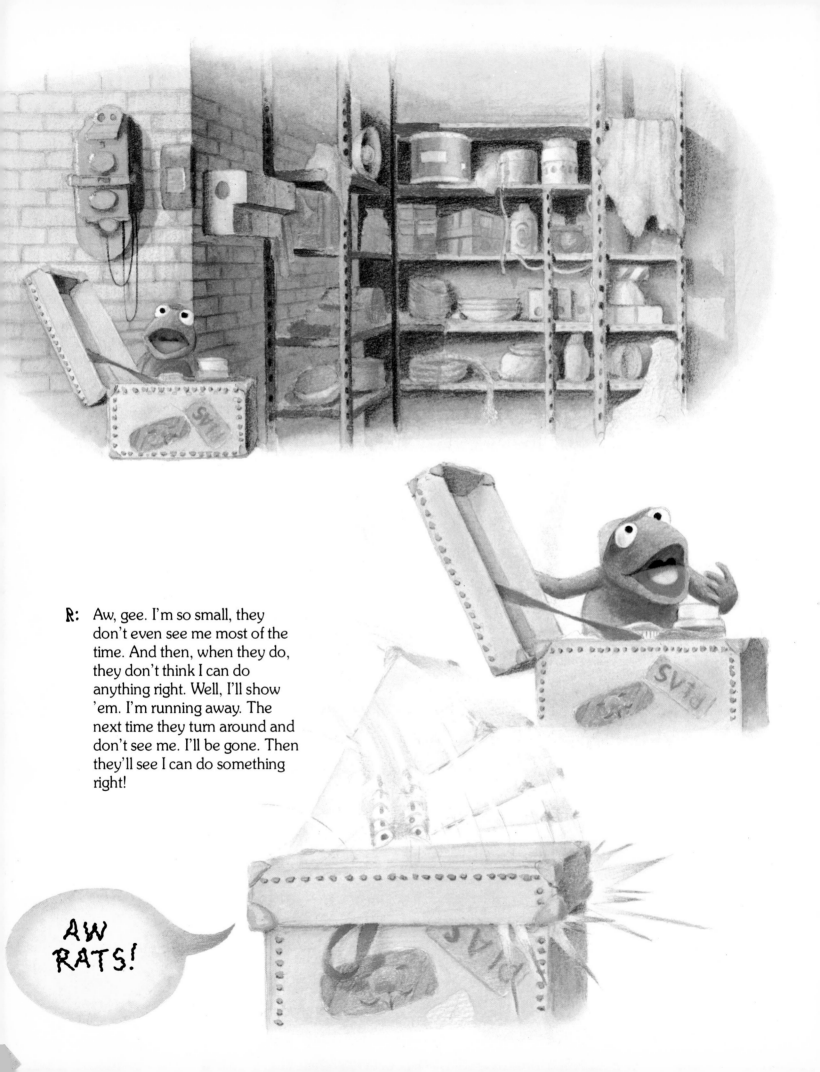

R: Aw, gee. I'm so small, they
don't even see me most of the
time. And then, when they do,
they don't think I can do
anything right. Well, I'll show
'em. I'm running away. The
next time they turn around and
don't see me. I'll be gone. Then
they'll see I can do something
right!

AW RATS!

(later . . .)

R: Say, listen, can I do a song on the show tonight?

K: Oh, funny you should mention it, Robin. You know, I was just thinking the same thing.

R: Oh boy! Look, the way I see it, the curtain opens and I'm standing there in a spotlight. The music swells and I sing: AWAY OUT HERE, THEY'VE GOT A NAME …

K: Oh, no no no no no no! "They Call the Wind Maria"!

R: Yeah, great, huh?

K: Er, Robin, that's ridiculous. No, no, no, listen. I have a cute little song here that's much more fitting to a frog your age. It's called "I'm Five."

R: It's called cute and yucky. I don't wanna do it.

K: O.K. Forget it.

R: Oh, hey. Is that any way to treat a performer? I'm gonna get an agent! I'm gonna get a lawyer!

K: Er, I'm gonna get your father.

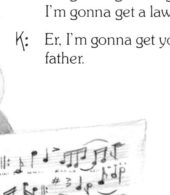

R: I'm gonna get right out and learn this cute little song.

K: And now, ladies and gentlemen, Robin is
   going to sing for us a cute little song called
   "I'm Five."

R: *(Singing)* I'm five, I'm five!
   I'm a big frog now, I'm five.
   I can dress myself
   I don't need mum to help me anymore …

AWAY OUT HERE...

J.P. BRINGS DOWN THE HOUSE

Scooter: Oh, Kermit, you know my uncle?

J.P. Grosse: Yeah, I own the theater. The ground it stands on, and the mineral rights under it. In fact, I probably own you too, frog. *(To Scooter)* Kid, make a note. See if we own the frog. If not, take an option.

K: Er, well, J.P., I suppose you're here on an inspection tour?

J.P.: Yeah, you could call it that.

K: Well, attendance is up, revenue is up. Just about everything is up, Sir.

J.P.: Yeah, well the theater's coming down.

K: WHAT?

J.P.: I'm tearing it down. Putting in a junkyard.

K: B-b-but why?

J.P.: Because there's more money in real junk than this junk you got here. Scooter, c'mon kid, this well's dry. Er, don't forget the option on the frog. Get a lien on his legs. *(J.P. exits)*

K: I-I think my stock just dropped.

K: Ladies and gentlemen at this time we have a very special . . . uh, uh, look, I'm trying to make an introduction.

J.P.: Aw, go ahead. I'm just checking the floor.

K: Uh, ladies and gentlemen . . .

J.P.: Make a note, some of these boards are rotten.

K: Oh, that's too bad.

J.P.: You know, if you'd dry your flippers before you came out here this wouldn't happen.
(J.P. exits)

K: Oh. Uh, uh . . . ladies and gentlemen . . .

J.P.: Yeah, well, I'm tearing the theater down. Putting in a junkyard. Hmm, yeah, course I will.

MP: Oh, oh, look . . . it's Scooter's uncle, the famous J.P. Grosse. Oh, I had no idea that someone so rich could be so good-looking.

J.P.: *(Ignoring Piggy)* . . . Yeah, listen, I don't want excuses, just get the widow's wheelchair!

MP: Hello, my name is Miss Piggy, the singing star of The Muppet Show.

J.P.: *(On phone)* . . . Well, sue then.

MP: Er, I wonder, would you like to hear me sing?

J.P.: *(On phone)* Yeah, yeah, yeah . . .

MP: Oh, all right: Call me irresponsible
                Call me unreliable
                Call me . . .

J.P.: Call you . . . what for? No money in hog calling.

MP: Well, call this, cigar breath! H-I-I-I-Y-A-A!!

K: For a second there, I thought somebody was gonna get
hurt around here.

K: Oh, no . . . what am I going to do?

GONZO: Hi Kermit, what's happening?

K: Oh, Gonzo, haven't you heard the news?

G: No.

K: Scooter's uncle is going to tear down this theater.

G: NO!

K: Yes . . . he's going to build a junkyard on this very spot.

G: NO!

K: Yes.

G: Oh, what a TERRIFIC idea for an act!

K: WHAT?

G: I wish I'd thought of it . . .

K: There goes a real trouper.

K: Scooter!

S: What is it, Kermit?

K: You're the only one here who can talk your uncle out of tearing this theater down.

S: Oh, gee I, I don't think so, Kermit.

K: Sure you can. Appeal to his sense of art. Tell him about all the people who'll be out of work . . .

S: Sorry, Kermit.

K: . . . Including you.

S: Wait right here. Hey, Uncle J.P., you can't tear this theater down.

J.P.: Sure I can. I've got the junkyard all planned. Gonna put the old cars right here, and the old tires over there . . .

S: Uh, well, what about your sense of art?

J.P.: Art who?

S: Well, what will all these people do for money?

J.P.: Oh, let 'em spend cake.

S: But, what about me?

J.P.: Oh, well, I was going to put you in charge of the junkyard. What do you say to that, kid?

Let's get started, Uncle Partner!

SCOOTER!

K: Well, we made it through another show. And, er, I am very glad, you know, mostly because this may be our last show. You see, Scooter's uncle still wants to tear this place down.

(J.P. enters)

J.P.: No, cancel that plan. I'm not going to tear this place down.

K: You're not?

J.P.: Nah, it'd be a waste of money. This stuff is going to fall in by itself. Look at this floor!

PUPPETS & COSTUMES BY

Amy Van Gilder	John Lovelady
Caroly Wilcox	Faz Fazakas
Mari Kaestle	Larry Jameson
Dave Goelz	Rollin Krewson

Calista Hendrickson
and
Bonnie Erickson

SPECIAL PUPPETS BY

Don Sahlin

DESIGN CONSULTANT

Michael K. Frith

The Muppet Performers

FEATURING

Frank Oz as: Miss Piggy
Fozzie Bear
Animal
Sam the Eagle
Marvin Suggs
George the Janitor*

with

Jerry Nelson as: Sgt. Floyd Pepper
Robin the Frog
J.P. Grosse
Dr. Julius Strangepork
Uncle Deadly
Crazy Harry*

Richard Hunt as: Scooter
Statler
Beaker
Sweetums
Janice*

Dave Goelz as: The Great Gonzo
Dr. Bunsen Honeydew
Muppy
Zoot*

Erin Ozker as: Hilda
(and sometimes Janice)

John Lovelady as: Nigel
(and sometimes Crazy Harry)

and

Jim Henson as: Kermit the Frog
Rowlf
Dr. Teeth
Capt. Link Hogthrob
The Newsman
The Swedish Chef (with Frank Oz)
Waldorf
Mahna Mahna*

*plus assorted chickens, cows, pigs, dogs, Whatnots,
Frackles, Koozebanes, Snowths, Heaps and unnamable Hairy Things

STATLER: Well, now that you've seen *The Muppet Show Book,* how do you like it?

WALDORF: What? Oh, *(yawns)* . . . I wasn't paying attention. Ah, what was it about?

S: It was about 190 pages, you old fool.